Psychology, The Machine, and Society

LEONARD CARMICHAEL

SEVENTH ANNUAL

ARTHUR DEHON LITTLE MEMORIAL LECTURE

AT THE

MASSACHUSETTS INSTITUTE OF TECHNOLOGY

At Cambridge, Massachusetts, November 17, 1953

Inaugural Little Memorial Lecture, *Science, Government and Industry*, Sir Edward V. Appleton, к.с.в., November 19, 1946

Second Little Memorial Lecture, *Physics in the Contemporary World*, J. Robert Oppenheimer, November 25, 1947

Third Little Memorial Lecture, *Research on a Single Reaction and its Social Effects*, Robert E. Wilson, November 23, 1948

Fourth Little Memorial Lecture, *The Unity of the Sciences and the Humanities*, Detlev W. Bronk, November 22, 1949

Fifth Little Memorial Lecture, *Social Change and Scientific Progress*, William C. Menninger, May 1, 1951

Sixth Little Memorial Lecture, *Science and Democracy*, Sir Henry Tizard, November 5, 1951

Seventh Little Memorial Lecture, *Psychology, the Machine, and Society*, Leonard Carmichael, November 17, 1953

The Arthur Dehon Little Memorial Lectureship

THE Arthur Dehon Little Memorial Lectureship was established in 1944 with funds donated by Arthur D. Little, Inc.,
in memory of its founder. The dislocation of normal activities
at the Institute owing to the war made it impossible to inaugurate
the lectures until 1946, when the first of the lectures was given
by Sir Edward V. Appleton, Secretary of the Department of Scientific and Industrial Research, an agency of the British Government.
He lectured on the subject, "Science, Government and Industry."
The lecturers and the subjects of subsequent lectures are listed on
the facing page.

The broad purpose of the lectureship is to promote interest
in and stimulate discussion of the social implications inherent in
the development of science, through lectures delivered upon
invitation by distinguished contributors to the advancement of
science and the arts.

It is the purpose of the lectureship to secure the record of the
deepest thoughts and convictions of our lecturers, based on many
years of experience in their contacts with science, society, government, economics, and the humanities. It is appropriate that this
should be, because of the extraordinary breadth of vision of Dr.
Little, in whose honor the lectureship was founded.

Psychology, the Machine, and Society

LAST SPRING in the sky over Korea when a pilot in one of our fast jet planes sighted an enemy jet approaching, he had to respond quickly, if at all. The human eye-nerve-muscle system requires at least one-fifth of a second to operate after such stimulation. If a directional movement trend in another plane is to be estimated, a much longer time is needed. During the period required for effective human response, two jets move hundreds of feet from where they were when the stimulation was initiated. In 1909 at the first Gordon-Bennett Air Race the winning plane averaged just over 47 miles per hour. Today plane speeds of more than fifteen times this rate are not uncommon, whereas the average speed of the operation of the human sense organs, brain, and muscles has not changed in these years. Indeed, it is very doubtful whether the best human reaction time of an ace pilot of the Korean war was different from that of a leading archer of the New Stone Age, when the bow and arrow had just been developed by the neolithic counterpart of our Atomic Energy Commission.

There is thus a hard reality behind some of the present-day lurid science fiction: Men have now made machines that are challenging the inborn anatomical and mental limitations of their masters. Furthermore, in the past few years increase in speed of travel, ease of world communication, potential military destructiveness, and eradication and control of disease have violently upset the slowly evolved balance of the ages between the individual and his material and social world.

[5]

These facts emphasized the need for a scientific consideration of man's fixed and sometimes inborn physiological and psychological capacities, in relation to novel and ingenious machines, to newly released energy sources, and especially to political and economic systems that are now so rapidly transforming the world.

Man has studied and speculated about his nature for many centuries. Probably ever since he first saw his reflection in a prehistoric pool he has wondered about himself. Throughout the ages, theologians, lawyers, physicians, philosophers, poets, myth-makers, and more recently anthropologists, psychiatrists, geneticists, physiologists, sociologists, and many other specialists, as well as psychologists, have pondered aspects of the great question "What is man?" None has yet produced the final answer. Not even the most ardent present-day advocates of the usefulness of psychology would dream of maintaining that this one area of study alone can ever give a full reply to this obdurate riddle of the Sphinx. Nevertheless, modern experimental psychology has developed useful techniques and is providing factual, fundamental information about human nature. The present-day relationship between human beings and machines and society is being made more understandable by this science in more than a few respects. When the student of mental reactions is asked, "What are the capacities of human individuals?" his answer today is far from complete, but it is possible to approach an answer in modest, factual terms.

The wise psychologist does not attempt to predict the nature of the end products of human artistic creation, or try to determine the boundaries of man's highest intellectual potentialities or spiritual and esthetic insights. Rather, psychologists try to describe, wherever possible in quantitative terms, basic mental processes, which are often shown to be related to the anatomical and physiological living machinery of a unique primate called *Homo sapiens*.

Many questions similar to the following can be asked and to a limited degree answered by scientific psychology: "What is the average difference between man's fastest reaction to a sound and to a light?" "How fast and how accurately can different human individuals learn specific items of information, such as series of numbers?" "How rapidly does forgetting of specific new associations take place?" "How do individuals vary in the composite of abilities, sometimes called intelligence?" "What are the typical changes in the expression of emotion as an individual grows from babyhood to adult life?" "What is the effect of sleep deprivation on skilled motor performance?" "How is language related to thought?"

The extent of new knowledge in this field is illustrated by a *Handbook of Human Engineering Data* recently published by Tufts College psychologists under contract with the Navy. This book, which has the external dimensions of the New York City telephone directory, is a compilation of the present state of useful psychological facts about the measurable traits and abilities of human beings. Its pages give hundreds of tables and graphs representing the results of experimental study of specific aspects of mental capacity. Many of the tables show averages and also give extremes of variation. In such studies of human mental characteristics, individual differences are recognized as important. There is no more firmly established fact about men, women, and children than that variation is the most invariable law of nature. The amazing range of human capacity in any population is one of the first facts

[7]

to be recognized by one who is concerned with making better machines for human operators or even with speculation about social, political, or economic theory or reform.

In general, therefore, the information made available as a result of experimental psychology is essential to concrete thinking concerning the present-day changing relationships between man and his world. The engineer who builds a new Diesel locomotive is limited by the properties of the materials he uses. The weight, strength, heat resistance, elasticity, and other characteristics of the metals he employs do not predetermine the shape into which the material is to be fabricated. On the other hand, parts of such engines cannot be made of metals that have other than very specific characteristics. The same relationship holds for one who would consider how modern machines and present-day society are related to the inborn traits of every human being. "Which of you by taking thought can add one cubit unto his stature?" also applies to other characteristics besides height. The jet pilot, already referred to, cannot by thought, education, or wishing speed up beyond a certain fixed point the time his nerves must take in responding to external stimuli. Anyone concerned with designing new airplanes or with training pilots to fly such planes in formations, or with developing a better political or economic system, must not forget that physiologically and psychologically men have a large number of inborn capacities and many specific limitations.

As a first conclusion of this paper, therefore, may it be suggested that a modern and effective understanding of man will certainly involve a number of levels of study? Among the types of information that will be required in considering man's complex relationships to his total environment will be as accurate as possible a knowledge of the basic makeup of human beings.

This point of view was well expressed by Dr. Arthur D. Little, in whose honor this lecture is named. He wrote, "Since most of the troubles that beset mankind have their origin in human nature, it would seem worth the while of those who make laws to study and apply the findings of the biologists and psychologists as to what human nature really is and what are the springs of its motivation." Though this was written twenty-five years ago, it is even more clearly true today than it was then.

Much more research in basic scientific psychology is therefore an urgent need of our age. "If only," says Professor I. A. Richards, "something could be done in psychology remotely comparable to what has been achieved in physics, practical consequences might be expected even more remarkable than any that the engineer can contrive. The first positive steps in the science of the mind have been slow in coming, but they are beginning to change man's whole outlook." Our educational system, too, may well be planned so that proper and adequate training in psychology may be given and so that enough able young men and women in each generation are allowed an opportunity to become experts in this field. Experimental psychology and human engineering have contributions to make to machine design and, what is more important, even to social understanding.

Let us now look at the second noun of our title, *the machine*. Many of the pleasant and interesting, as well as many of the alarming, characteristics of our age are a direct result of machines and of other new processes and procedures following upon man's growing understanding of pure and applied science. The past fifteen decades have seen more developments which are based on quantitative and exact methods of studying nature than all preceding ages of history. During this period, in such societies as ours, science has made possible the release of man from drudgery in ways that were previously unthinkable. New sources of energy, and now atomic power itself, have been substituted for the old inefficient and painful work of human or animal muscles. Some great periods of the past were based upon the forced labor of mute human slaves. Today, machines, our new and willing servants, relieve us from much of the relentless work that was accepted as inevitable by the unbroken line of our toiling ancestors.

Novel electronic systems are today being developed, for example, here at the Massachusetts Institute of Technology, which will further lift the curse of drudgery not only from man's biceps and triceps but even from his mind. If human beings by their social blundering do not bring on war or political chaos and thus capriciously spoil this process, we may logically hope that the technology of the present and future will be even more humanly valuable than it has been in the past. It must be remembered also that advances in medicine and public health in the last generation have been without precedent. The average length of life has been increased and human beings have been relieved in an almost unbelievable way from much of their physical suffering, which, like muscular toil, had always before been accepted as the inevitable lot of all sons and daughters of Adam.

The support of research in pure and applied physical and biological science is for this reason doubly imperative. If society is to operate efficiently the best modern psychological and personnel procedures must be used to discover in each generation those individuals who are best qualified to be educated so that they may in their turn carry on effective research and development in these fields. Such able individuals should also be encouraged to undergo the self-discipline and the training in mathematics and other basic fields of study required of those who are to do real research in science. This kind of preparation is absolutely essential to those who would wisely direct and maintain as well as develop the machines, processes, and services on which the modern world depends. Nature does not provide enough children in each generation who have outstanding mathematical and other academic aptitudes, as well as the personality characteristics necessary to become true modern scientists, to allow any to be wasted. It has been suggested that creative research of the highest order in the quantitative physical sciences can be expected only from selected individuals in the upper two percent of the population in measured intellectual ability. Such rare and valuable talent bearers should be nurtured and helped to use their inborn capacities for the welfare of our scientifically based age. The world cannot afford to squander its scientific manpower! It is particularly wasteful of human resources when individuals, recognized as singularly talented and perhaps well trained in certain scientific or technical specialties, are allowed or required either in military or civilian life to perform tasks that others can do as well or even better.

Dr. Arthur D. Little, again, saw with peculiar clarity the need of fostering able scientists. Men of science constituted for him a separate Fifth Estate in society. He said in a memorable paragraph, "This Fifth Estate is composed of those having the simplicity to wonder, the ability to question, the power to generalize, the capacity to apply. It is, in short, the company of thinkers, workers, expounders, and practitioners upon which the world is absolutely dependent for the preservation and advancement of that organized knowledge called science."

As a second conclusion of this paper, then, it may be suggested that society should give full attention to the discovery of human talent and to the effective education of promising leaders in pure and applied science and, it may be added, in other worthwhile scholarly fields. That all men are not born equally able to use mathematics is but one of many facts that must be accepted by those who are to plan wisely for the education of our youth for effective service to society.

From time to time we hear proposed the monstrous notion that a moratorium on scientific research should be established. Those who make such suggestions mistakenly blame science for our present social ills. Can anyone, however, with clear eyes doubt that the world now needs more, not less, science, and a wider, not more restricted, recognition of its true implications and importance?

Men ask over and over again: Why have human beings, who have made such good machines and such progress in understanding the cause and cure of many human illnesses, failed in creating a just and stable national and world social order? The author of this paper knows that he cannot answer this great question, but he still believes that it is worthy of the best thought of all of us. In the first place, the fact that the world has not yet developed a thoroughly workable political and economic organization cannot be blamed upon the failure of many men to consider the matter. For centuries philosophers, statesmen, political scientists, aspiring dictators, and even glittering soldiers of fortune like Napoleon have thought and talked about the need for social and political change and improvement on a world-wide scale. Sometimes it almost seems that society has suffered not so much because it has failed to consider its own improvement but rather because it has been tampered with by too many would-be reformers. Many of these advocates of social change have not understood or wanted to understand what we have called in this paper the basic nature of human beings.

The kind of thinking that has been so triumphantly successful in developing purely mechanical systems has not always worked when applied hastily to man's relationship to man. Edmund Burke, who was certainly one of the outstanding political scientists and philosophers of the eighteenth century, emphasized this fact. He spoke of ignorant men who were not fools enough to meddle with their own clocks but who still felt free to advocate the taking apart of society and the disrupting of its immemorial springs, balance, counteractions, and cooperating powers.

For years sociologists have said that in some respects society is like an organism. This analogy may be carried too far, but it does seem to be true that in old and well-established communities there is an almost organic unity in the structural pattern of social living. Successful modern physicians do not try to create new organisms in the place of the patients they are called upon to treat. Medicine rather has learned to alter the processes that interfere with health and to recognize that a real cure is usually the result of restorative processes inherent in the body. These processes may be thought of as part of the body itself and have been produced by millions of years of organic evolution. This approach of the modern medical scientist may have a lesson for the social and economic reformer. Today, however, looking back at the social changes that have been advocated in the relatively few years since the French Revolution, one can hardly escape the conclusion that would-be social doctors have all too often tried to put together a new society and not to cure the old one. They seem not to have realized that some aspects of man's social organization, like the human species itself, have grown by the slow evolution of possibly a million years of man's living with man on this planet. Some inborn and essentially unchanging physiological and psychological characteristics of the human organism make certain social patterns more effective than others.

Social advances in recorded history there certainly have been. Democracy as we know it at its best is an example of such progress in man's estate. The abolition, in most parts of the world, of human slavery is another sure advance. It is distressing to realize, however, as we think of both democracy and the abolition of slavery, that we are living in an age in which new patterns of dictatorship and of human servitude are again being fostered by some of those who talk most loudly about creating society on a new mechanical plan.

In view of our present world conditions it is surprising to remember that many of our academic parents and grandparents convinced themselves that all or almost all social change of any sort was real social progress. Many of them had a simple faith that various types of social disruption, which they advocated, would lead to social uplift for the benefit of mankind everywhere. Some Victorian intellectual leaders adopted uncritically what now seems to have been a deceptively attractive general idea. They looked at the most external aspects of Darwinian biological evolutionary theory and then suggested that the same factors which were assumed to have operated during millions of years in the development of species of plants and animals could be counted on in a few decades of human planning, or telic social evolution, to establish a wholly new society. These reformers never dreamed of the difficulties in our age that have followed the social upheaval they did so much to promote. In nineteenth-century England many academic reformers cheered politely as the age-old influence of the Established Church and of religion in general was being undermined. They saw only good in the passing of the remnants of the ancient stratification of society. Their eyes were closed to the fact that many of those born to so-called special privilege traditionally recognized that they had inherited, along with the rights and status of their class, certain inescapable social obligations. The reformers who rejoiced most at the passing of the established order did not foresee that the theory of social change they advocated would later be stretched to justify a police state and the denial of human personal liberties.

As Dr. Russell Kirk has recently sagaciously and persuasively pointed out, from the time of the French Revolution on there have been those who have seen the dangers inherent in unbridled social change. John Adams, our second President, was such a philosopher. So was the often misunderstood English statesman Disraeli, and in a very different way Matthew Arnold. There have been many others. In more recent times George Santayana, Irving Babbitt, Paul Elmer More, T. S. Eliot, and Peter Viereck have made clear some of the errors in much of the thinking of the socialists, collectivists, and disrupters generally.

Jeremy Bentham, John Stuart Mill, and other utilitarians and Fabian socialists were great hands at suggesting how, Humpty-Dumpty-like, human society could be broken apart. It now seems that they, like all the king's horses and all the king's men, were not equally good at suggesting means by which the organic structure of our slowly evolved society could again be regenerated after it had been shattered. Not a few modern thinkers agree, and with some reason, that our civilized world owes many of its worst disorders to the verbal blandishments of the romantic writings of Rousseau. Certainly few philosophers ever espoused a more unrealistic psychology of human nature than did this brilliant vagabond and revolutionary thinker. After the fall of the old regime in France a whole succession of dreamers, utopians, and sentimental socialists in various countries, often explicitly influenced by Rousseau, advocated turning many of the established laws and principles of society upside down. The idea that a freely competitive economy is a high expression of man's inborn nature seems currently to be gaining ground as the practical impossibilities of the so-called class-less society of socialism or communism are disclosed. That the legal sanctity of private property is a prime guarantee of our human freedoms is probably better recognized today than at any other time in the past century.

Even the late Maynard Keynes, not always the most conservative of economists, recognized the point of view here being considered. Dr. Kirk, in his recent admirable book *The Conservative Mind,* quotes Keynes as saying, "Benthamism I do now regard as the worm which has been gnawing at the insides of modern civilization and is responsible for its present moral decay. We used to regard the Christians as the enemy, because they appeared as the representatives of tradition, convention, and hocus-pocus. In truth it was the Benthamite calculus, based on over-valuation of the economic criterion, which was destroying the quality of the popular ideal." Kirk summarized Keynes as asserting that "the final *reductio ad absurdum* of Benthamism is known as Marxism; drained of spirit and imagination by the gross objectives of the utilitarians, we have ended defenseless before this brutal descendant of Bentham's philanthropy."

In many places today therefore a new conviction is growing that what ails our age is not some ancient political, economic, or social cancer, but rather a loss of the old understanding that virtue in the individuals who make up society is basic in creating a good, a just, a free, and above all an achieving social order. The rash theorists and self-seeking politicians who have attacked existing organic social orders have often sneered at this age-old idea. For example, many of the self-styled liberals of the nineteenth century believed that a society could exist without religion, but this assumption has never been demonstrated through a series of generations. They also underestimated the importance of the slowly evolved traditional wisdom of mankind and the power of custom, that universal gyroscope of society, in the effective control of human beings and especially in the ordering of the lives of those having limited capacity in the use of abstract verbal principles. Practical ideals and a fixed scale of human values were recognized, taught, and acclaimed, if not always lived up to, by the old system. Politeness and courtesy, sometimes called the minor morals or the lubricants of society, also were handed down from the past to make social living more pleasant. All too often these intangible and in some respects truly spiritual characteristics of man's ancient mores were thrown out by the sudden would-be reformers with their superficially mechanistic ideas. There were, to be sure, injustices and inequities in all the old orders of society. But those who saw reform as the mere provision of more and more superficial entertainment and greater and greater idleness for larger and larger groups of people were set, it now appears, on copying the worst and not the best of the old society they were trying to overturn. As hours of work were decreased and pay increased, the economic feasibility of skilled handwork and its consequent artistic satisfactions to the worker were largely lost. It is a sad commentary that sometimes this precious and potentially valuable new leisure has been occupied by activities no more constructive than wagering on dogs as they run after mechanical rabbits.

Thus we return to the strange fact that men who have learned to release atomic energy, to bounce signals back and forth from the moon, to banish typhoid and yellow fevers, and to make electronic calculators do the work of tired brains have failed to maintain the best intrinsic satisfactions, the highest ancient ethical and moral values and spiritual insights in a changing society. It is all too clear that some of the would-be doctors of society, unlike modern scientific physicians, have failed to recognize that human beings are not all alike and that they have inborn characteristics and limitations that must be taken into consideration by those who would effectively improve society.

We are forced back to the conclusion that the basic psychology of those parts of human nature that are inborn ought not to be disregarded by the successful social engineer any more than the properties of metals can be disregarded by one who plans to construct a good television receiver. As Lewis Mumford once put it in an address before the American Association for the Advancement of Science, "The tendency to overlook the human end which our automatic organizations serve has begun to pervade our whole civilization; and in the end, if it is uncorrected, it may effectually undermine our best achievements. . . . No matter how marvelous our inventions, how productive our industries, how exquisitely automatic our machines, the whole process may be brought to a standstill by its failure to engage the human personality or to serve its needs."

Radical social reformers have often ignored or even tried to pretend that biological heredity was not important in psychology. William Godwin, a most fixed-eyed and unrealistic but strangely influential social reformer of the late eighteenth century, believed in the perfectibility of the human race in one generation provided the environment could only be changed in the right way. Many later reformers have unthinkingly accepted this view. Even the great John Stuart Mill suggested that anyone who believed in inherited traits was an advocate of social reaction. In our own time this old scientific heresy, that inborn differences between men of the sort measured by aptitude tests do not exist, is still proclaimed as a new truth in Russia. In holding this position at least at the verbal level the steel-handed present-day Russian Communists are walking in the path of the visionary nineteenth-century melioristic reformers who preceded them. Intelligence tests in education are now proscribed by Moscow. Such measuring devices are said to demonstrate differences that cannot exist in the so-called perfect environment of a communist state. It would be interesting to know through what back door a realistic recognition of inborn individual differences is now introduced in Russian education. That such differences exist in Russia as well as in America is as sure as is the existence of chromosomes. It is true, of course, that modern psychology must deal with both inborn and culturally determined traits, for ordinarily both chromosomal determination and environmental forces cooperate in producing each physical or mental performance of every person. But to ignore inherited differences in individuals is to close one's eyes to most important facts.

Is it not fair to say, therefore, that a major mistake of the superficially mechanistic reformers of society has been their inability to recognize that society is made up of individual free organisms with conservative and yet varying brains and muscles? To put this in another way, is not a good society made up of bad individual men impossible? Certainly this is true, in spite of the satirical arguments of such tongue-in-cheek philosophers as Bernard de Mandeville who have attempted to assert that private vices make public benefits. A group of people of varying inborn abilities but alike in trying hard to be honest, unselfish, charitable, virtuous, diligent, self-reliant, and full respecters of private property would not need to worry too much about external social or economic reform.

This point of view makes it clear that what Peter Viereck has well called the "revolt against revolt" should now challenge our full attention. Have we not been living too long in a world that has tried to pretend that social upheaval is always social progress? Destructive social reformers often have sweet tasting and mysterious medicines to propose. Such men in our time begin by suggesting new legislation that seems to give something for nothing. Harold Laski, for example, always could attack what he called "privilege" as he advocated more socialization of industry. Envy may for a time be a satisfactory motive to be used by the selfish demagogue to get votes, but it is a bad sentiment on which to build a stable and achieving society. When legislation does not produce the results hoped for by the reformers more and more police enforcement is demanded. Those, however, who see that the organic structure of society must be maintained and slowly made better by improving the personal character of individual human beings are at a disadvantage in combating the schemes of the advocates of wholesale and destructive social change. Those who believe in self-discipline first have no simple and easy patent medicine to prescribe. All that such conservative and true reformers can suggest is a firmer adherence by more people to the highest ethical and religious teachings and more of the right sort of education fitted for individuals of differing interests and inborn talents. Social improvement of this sort is usually within the reach of every individual, but it requires first the hard work of self-reform and not the iconoclastic fun of pulling down others who externally seem more fortunate or who have been more diligent and thrifty.

When we think here of the training of individuals let us not forget that the objectives of education are in the last analysis socially determined. In our political democracy and our tested and effective, competitive, free, capitalist economy we all have a responsibility to see to it that our schools foster an education that makes possible the discovery of truth and the achievement of individual intellectual liberty. Harvard University's now justly famous book *General Education in a Free Society* wisely begins with these words of Plato, "Youth is the time when the character is being molded and easily takes any impress one may wish to stamp on it. Shall we then simply allow our children to listen to any stories that anyone happens to make up and so receive into their minds ideas often the very opposite to those we shall think they ought to have when they are grown up?"

If this statement from the *Republic* is accepted we are today challenged to re-examine the question as to whether, under the influence of a shallow and often misunderstood positivism and an incomplete naturalism, American education has not in the past generation turned too sharply away from all instruction that had as its aim the inculcation of fixed systems of values. If a free and stable society depends on citizens who act as they do because they are trying hard to live up to high ethical standards, then let us do what we can to raise up new generations that know what these standards and scales of values are.

It is easier, of course, to talk about the teaching of ethical and even esthetic values than to say how such instruction should be given in a free democracy. Certainly, however, an education aiming to accomplish such ends will emphasize studies that acquaint the members of each new generation with the true wisdom of the race concerning the best ways in which men can react to one another. The study of biology, anthropology, sociology, economics, political science, social history, psychiatry, and psychology will help in providing a basis for this understanding. But these fields alone will not provide the needed humanistic value scales because in their very nature these sciences must be objective and factual.

[22]

The conclusion seems forced upon us with new inevitability, therefore, that an education which is to make free, sensitive, socially responsible individuals with self-accepted value systems must emphasize the great body of studies, such as religion, law, history, and literature, that represents the noblest human wisdom of the past — "the best that has been thought and said in the world." To put this in another way, it seems that the education of individuals who are to have the persistence, the courage, and the stamina to reform themselves before they try to reform society will require a sympathetic study of the best parts of those strands of our intellectual tradition which we call the humanities.

This conclusion, of course, is not novel. Students here at the Massachusetts Institute of Technology are naturally and most properly offered unsurpassed opportunities to study the physical sciences and the whole range of modern applied technologies. In recent years, however, under the far-sighted educational statesmanship of former President Karl T. Compton and now of President James R. Killian, Jr., this world-renowned scientific research institution has emphasized basic instruction in the humanities. Thus an effort is made to have students here become not only scientists and technologists but also wise human beings who understand the intellectual, artistic, and spiritual traditions and values that mankind has gradually beaten out for itself through the ages. This fortunately is a point of view in higher education that today is sweeping to new recognition everywhere in America. The old destructive educational revolution of the last generation that tried to banish values from school and college work is being unmasked as a destroyer of much that was of first importance to a stable and achieving society.

In this great institution, and in others like it that are hospitable to many foreign students, it is good that this new point of view is being emphasized. Visiting students from other lands and cultures should not only be given our mathematical, scientific, and technological skills but also should learn the true spiritual wisdom of our free western world at its best.

Therefore, in recapitulation, as we think of psychology, the machine, and society, a few basic conclusions emerge. Science in a most general sense has given great sections of modern man a high standard of living and an opportunity to provide himself a life of health and comfort undreamed of in any ancient utopia. Further progress of this kind may be confidently expected if social and international disorder does not prevent it. Modern psychology, although still far from being able to provide final answers to all relevant questions, does show that man's understanding of his inborn and acquired make-up is important for technology and an understanding of society.

In spite of these demonstrated advances, pessimism about society is a dominant attitude of many thoughtful people in our day. Recent social upheavals aggravate this gloomy stand. Is it not conceivable, however, that in their faith in the possibility of social progress, Victorian intellectual leaders were nearer the truth than are some of our modern writers?

Man's mammalian characteristics are millions of years old, but man as a free intelligence is built to live in the future. The pilots of the atomic-powered airplanes of the year 3000 will have essentially the same conservative brains and muscles that our fathers possessed. Nevertheless, our growing knowledge of psychology, the machine, and society seems ready to help us make such future pilots and others of their generation ethically and socially wiser and more satisfied with life than we are. If we are to approach this better state it seems clear that we must be prepared to spend more money and thought than in the past on improving the quality of the instruction we offer to all the youth of our race. If we hope to have a finer, and more achieving society, education fitted to the aptitudes of each individual is a most promising tool. As we plan for the future place of education in our social order, let us have the courage to act as though we believe that the golden age is ahead and not behind!

Dr. Leonard Carmichael

AS a psychologist interested in applying the methods of his
science to the problems of behavior, Dr. Leonard Carmichael
has directed his talents over an amazingly wide range of investiga-
tion and endeavor. When he was a young instructor at Princeton
University in the 1920's he was concerned with the early development of behavior in the salamander. During World War II, as a
distinguished college president at Tufts, he was director of the
National Roster of Scientific and Specialized Personnel, the catalog
of America's scientists and specialists.

Leonard Carmichael was born in Philadelphia and attended
the Germantown Friends School in that city. It was natural that
his undergraduate training should be at Tufts College where his
maternal grandfather was Dean of the School of Religion. It was
to this alma mater that he returned as President in 1938, after
serving for two years as Dean of the Faculty at the University
of Rochester.

As an undergraduate biology student at Tufts he became interested in the physiology of the sense organs. This study led him to
psychology, and to graduate work at Harvard where he obtained
the degree of Doctor of Philosophy in 1924. After a year in Ger-
many as a Sheldon Traveling Fellow he joined the Department
of Psychology at Princeton. This appointment was followed by
his election to the chairmanship of the Department of Psychology
at Brown University, which institution he left in 1936 to become
Dean of the Faculty at the University of Rochester.

His appreciation of the importance of individual variability is
reflected in his scientific researches as well as in his dealings with
his fellow men. His skills and experience can find no more appropriate expression than in his present position of Secretary of the
Smithsonian Institution, a post he assumed on January 1, 1953.

His colleagues in psychology and science have recognized his
achievements by electing him to the National Academy of Sciences,
to the American Philosophical Society and to the presidency of the
American Psychological Association.

ARTHUR MacGIBBON
Printer and Publisher   Boston